Opposites

Old and New

Siân Smith

Heinemann
LIBRARY

Chicago, Illinois

Edited by Siân Smith, Diyan Leake, and Brynn Baker
Designed by Tim Bond and Peggie Carley
Picture research by Elizabeth Alexander
Production by Victoria Fitzgerald
Originated by Capstone Global Library Ltd

Library of Congress Cataloging-in-Publication Data
ISBN 978-1-4846-0335-2 (paperback)
ISBN 978-1-4846-0350-5 (ebook PDF)

Acknowledgments
We would like to thank the following for permission to reproduce photographs: Alamy: milos luzanin, Getty Images: ballyscanlon, 5, 22a, Dave King, 13, lina, aidukaite, 8, NI QIN, 10; Shutterstock: A_Belov, Africa Studio, 17, Aleksandar Mijatovic, front cover right, Chamille White, 21 left, dinadesign, front cover left, drpnncpptak, 9, Ijansempoi, 21 right, Irantzu Arbaizagoitia, 6, back cover bottom, Jjustas, 18, Kemeo, 20 left, Milos Luzanin, 12, restyler, 20 right, Sretnaz, 4, 22b, back cover top

Every effort has been made to contact copyright holders of material reproduced in this book. Any omissions will be rectified in subsequent printings if notice is given to the publisher.

Contents

Old and New

These socks are **old**.

These socks are **new**.

Are these socks old or new?

The socks are new.

This clock is old.

This clock is new.

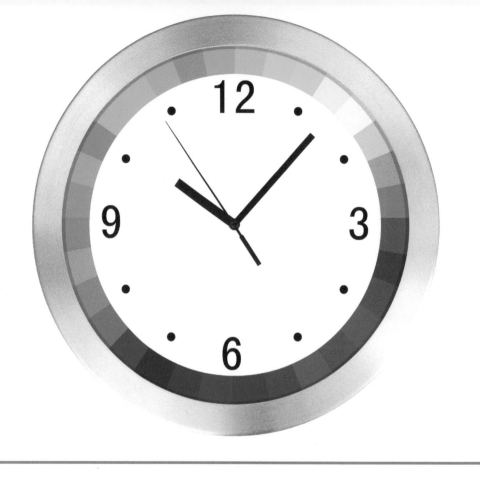

Is this clock old or new?

The
clock is
new.

The teddy bear is old.

The teddy bear is new.

Is this teddy bear old or new?

The teddy bear is old.

The book is old.

The book is new.

Is this book old or new?

The book is old.

Old and New Quiz

Which of these things are old?

Which of these things are new?

Answers on page 22

Picture Glossary

 **new** just made or begun

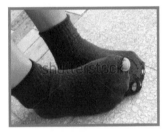 **old** has been used for a long time

Index

Answers to questions on pages 20 and 21

Left photo is old.

Right photo is new.

Notes for Teachers and Parents

BEFORE READING

Building background:

Ask children to think about something in their house that is new and something that is old.

AFTER READING

Recall and reflection:

Ask children if they like old or new things best. Do they like new clothes? New toys? Do they have some old toys that are their favorites? An old teddy bear or an old doll? Do we sometimes like old things best?

Sentence knowledge:

Help children find pages which have questions. How do they know?

Word knowledge (phonics):

Encourage children to point at the word *sock* on page 4. Sound out the three phonemes in the word *s/o/ck*. Ask children to sound out each phoneme as they point at the letters and then blend the sounds together to make the word *sock*. Challenge them to say some words that rhyme with *sock*. (clock, lock, knock, rock)

Word recognition:

Ask children to point at the word *book* on page 16.

AFTER-READING ACTIVITIES

Create a space on a bulletin board with a two-column chart with the columns labeled *Old* and *New*. Have children draw or cut out pictures of items both old and new to place on the display.

In This Book

Topic

old and new

Sentence stems

1. This is an old ___.
2. This ___ is new.
3. Is this ___ old or new?
4. This ___ is old.

High-frequency words

and

are

of

or

is

the

these

this

which